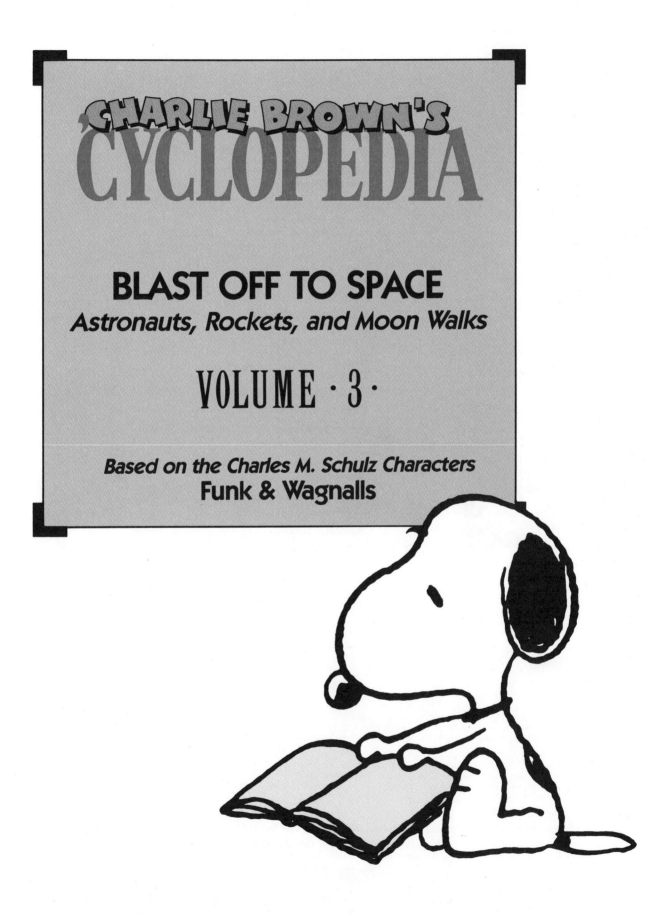

CHARLIE BROWN'S CYCLOPEDIA

BLAST OFF TO SPACE
Astronauts, Rockets, and Moon Walks

VOLUME · 3 ·

Based on the Charles M. Schulz Characters
Funk & Wagnalls

Charlie Brown's 'Cyclopedia
has been produced
by Mega-Books of New York,
Inc. in conjunction
with the editorial, design,
and marketing staff of
Field Publications.

STAFF FOR MEGA-BOOKS

Pat Fortunato
Editorial Director

Diana Papasergiou
Production Director

Susan Lurie
Executive Editor

Rosalind Noonan
Senior Editor

Adam Schmetterer
Research Director

**Michaelis/Carpelis
Design Assoc., Inc.**
Art Direction and Design

STAFF FOR FIELD PUBLICATIONS

Cathryn Clark Girard
Assistant Vice President,
Juvenile Publishing

Elizabeth Isele
Executive Editor

Kristina Jones
Executive Art Director

Leslie Erskine
Marketing Manager

Elizabeth Zuraw
Senior Editor

Michele Italiano-Perla
Group Art Director

Kathleen Hughes
Senior Art Director

Photograph and Illustration Credits:
Jet Propulsion Laboratory, 12; Howard Levy, 19; NASA 14, 19, 21, 23, 25, 26, 27, 28, 30, 31, 33, 36, 38, 39, 41, 44, 45, 46, 47, 48, 50, 52, 55, 56, 57, 58, 59; Mary Ellen Senor, 16, 20, 34, 40; Don Sparks/Image Bank, 54; United States Army, 35; UPI/Bettmann Newsphotos, 31, 32.

ISBN: 0-8374-0048-1

Part of the material in this volume was previously published in *Charlie Brown's Second Super Book of Questions and Answers*.

Funk & Wagnalls, founded in 1876, is the publisher of *Funk & Wagnalls New Encyclopedia*, one of the most widely owned home and school reference sets, and many other adult and juvenile educational publications.

INTRODUCTION

Welcome to volume 3 of *Charlie Brown's 'Cyclopedia!* Have you ever wondered how it feels to blast off in a spacecraft, or who was the first space traveler, or why your weight drops to zero in outer space? Charlie Brown and the rest of the *Peanuts* gang are here to help you find the answers to these questions and many more about space travel. Have fun!

CONTENTS

CHAPTER 1

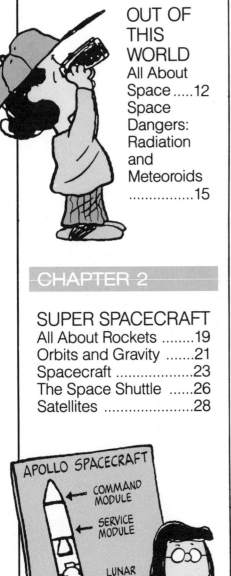

OUT OF THIS WORLD
All About Space 12
Space Dangers: Radiation and Meteoroids 15

CHAPTER 2

SUPER SPACECRAFT
All About Rockets 19
Orbits and Gravity 21
Spacecraft 23
The Space Shuttle 26
Satellites 28

CHAPTER 3

THREE CHEERS FOR ASTRONAUTS
Preparing Astronauts for Space Travel 31
Astronauts in Outer Space 31
Keeping Astronauts Healthy 36

CHAPTER 4

LIFT-OFF AND LANDING
NASA's Mission Control 38
3–2–1 Blast Off!.....39
Coming Back to Earth 40

CHAPTER 5

TAKE A WALK ON THE MOON
The First Moon Explorers 44
Getting Around on the Moon 47

CHAPTER 6

GET SET FOR THE FUTURE
Space Probes 50
Visiting Other Planets 51
Space Stations and Colonies 52

DID YOU KNOW?.....56

When you look up at the sky, what do you see? The Sun, the Moon, the stars. What mysteries lie beyond, millions and millions of miles away? Come and see different and exciting ways to travel through space. First let's learn some out-of-this-world facts about space.

OUT OF THIS WORLD

ALL ABOUT SPACE

What is space?

Space is the huge area beyond the cushion of air that surrounds the Earth. That cushion of air is called the atmosphere. The Earth's atmosphere gets very thin at about 60 miles up. There is no air left at 150 miles high.

Can you breathe in outer space?

No. There is no air in outer space, and you need to breathe air to stay alive. Space travelers need to carry a supply of air with them.

Is there an end to space?

Scientists don't know for sure. The part of outer space among the planets is called interplanetary (in-tur-PLAN-ih-ter-ee) space. Interplanetary space spreads out for about four billion miles. It includes the Earth and the other eight planets that travel around our Sun. The space beyond the farthest planets is called deep space. That is where the stars are. A huge group of these stars is called a galaxy. All the galaxies together are called the universe.

THE ANDROMEDA GALAXY

Are there sounds in outer space?

No. Sound is created when something vibrates—shakes back and forth quickly—in the air. These movements are called sound waves. They are sent out through the air to your ears. Then you hear the sound. Outer space has no air to shake up and carry sound waves, so you cannot hear any sounds.

Huge explosions are always taking place on the Sun. If there were air all the way from the Sun to the Earth, we would hear the roar of these explosions all the time!

Is outer space hot or cold?

Most of outer space is very cold—nearly 460 degrees below zero Fahrenheit. If you could travel to the space near a star, you would be warmer. Stars are like huge furnaces.

Heat streams out from them, warming up anything near them—including planets.

What can you expect to find in our solar system?

Our solar system is made up of the Sun, which is a star, as well as the Earth and the other eight planets that orbit the Sun. You'll also find asteroids, which are minor planets, and comets, which are frozen balls of gases.

Are there clouds in space?

There are clouds, but not like the ones near the Earth. Our clouds form when warm, moist air floats upward from the Earth and cools off. Some of that moisture then gathers into small water drops or bits of ice. Many of these drops of water and bits of ice together form a cloud. Most clouds are only a few miles above the ground.

In outer space, there is no water, so clouds of moisture cannot form. There are some huge clouds of gas and dust in deep space. They hide some of the distant stars from us. The clouds in space are called nebulas.

VIEW OF EARTH FROM SPACE

I OWN PROPERTY ON MARS!

Who owns outer space?

We all do! Most of the countries of the world have agreed that outer space should belong to everybody.

SPACE DANGERS: RADIATION AND METEOROIDS

What is radiation?

Scientists use the word radiation (ray-dee-AY-shun) for anything that flows outward—much like the spray of water from a garden hose. Like the water spray, radiation is made of tiny particles traveling in waves. One example of this is light streaming from the Sun or from a lamp. Another kind of radiation is heat. Heat is radiated from the Sun. Radio and television waves are sent out—or broadcast—through the air as streams of radiation. These waves are then picked up or received by our radios and TV's.

Is there radiation in outer space?

Yes, outer space is criss-crossed by many kinds of radiation. There are light waves. There are X rays, just like the ones the doctor uses to take pictures of your insides. There are other kinds of radiation, too. Radiation moves through space at about 186,000 miles per second.

Is radiation dangerous?

Exposure to some kinds of radiation is dangerous on Earth and in outer space. People cannot live if the radiation hits them directly. Radiation such as ultraviolet rays from the Sun can cause cancer and other health problems. On Earth, the atmosphere protects us from some of the Sun's harmful rays.

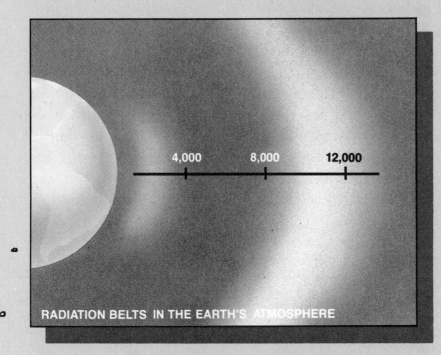

RADIATION BELTS IN THE EARTH'S ATMOSPHERE

What are radiation belts?

There are two invisible clouds around the Earth. They surround our planet like two belts looped around a ball. These clouds are called radiation belts. They are made up of tiny parts called electrons and protons—specks so small that you cannot see them, even under a microscope! Inside the belts, the radiation is weak. You would have to live within the belts for many years before any harm came to you.

What other dangers are there in space?

There are bits of rock called meteoroids (MEE-tee-uh-roidz) flying around in outer space. Many of them are no bigger than grains of sand. Some meteoroids are bits of material that never formed into planets. Some meteoroids can move hundreds of times faster than a rifle bullet. They can go so fast that even the smallest ones can do great damage to anything they hit.

A meteoroid that enters the Earth's atmosphere is called a meteor. If a meteor manages to reach the Earth's surface without burning up in the atmosphere, it is called a meteorite.

Another danger in space comes from space junk. These are the bits and pieces of material from old rockets and satellites that astronauts have left in outer space. Space junk orbits the Earth and can cause great damage to each new spacecraft that goes into orbit.

Tiny chips of paint from space junk have seriously damaged windows on our space shuttles!

CHAPTER 2

People have invented many ways to travel by air—airplanes and gliders, balloons and helicopters. All of these things can fly you around the world, but none of them can fly you out of this world and into outer space. If you want to soar through space, what you need is a rocket-powered spacecraft!

SUPER SPACECRAFT

ALL ABOUT ROCKETS

What is a rocket?

A rocket is a kind of engine, or motor, that can operate in space where there is no air. A rocket must be powerful enough to lift a very heavy spacecraft off the Earth. In order to do this, it burns special fuels.

Who made the first rocket?

Nobody knows exactly. The Chinese were using rockets more than 800 years ago. These rockets were powered by gunpowder. They were like the skyrockets that you see in Fourth of July fireworks shows.

In 1903, a Russian schoolteacher named Konstantin Tsiolkovsky (tzawl-KAWF-skee) had the idea of using rockets for flights into space. In 1926, the American scientist Robert H. Goddard sent up a rocket that went about as high as a 20-story building.

A Redstone 3 rocket launches a *Freedom 7* capsule into space. This astronaut in training is standing in front of a Mercury capsule.

19

How does a rocket work?

In order for something to move in one direction, it must give a push in the opposite direction. When you row a boat, you push the water in the opposite direction from the way you want to go. When you swim in a pool, you sometimes push back against the pool wall to move yourself forward.

   This kind of two-way action is what makes a rocket motor work. Fuel is burned inside the rocket. This is called "firing" the rocket. The burning fuel forms great clouds of hot gas. The heat makes the gases swell up so much that they need more room. They can escape only through an opening at the back of the rocket. Then, as the gases are forced out at the back, the spacecraft is pushed forward.

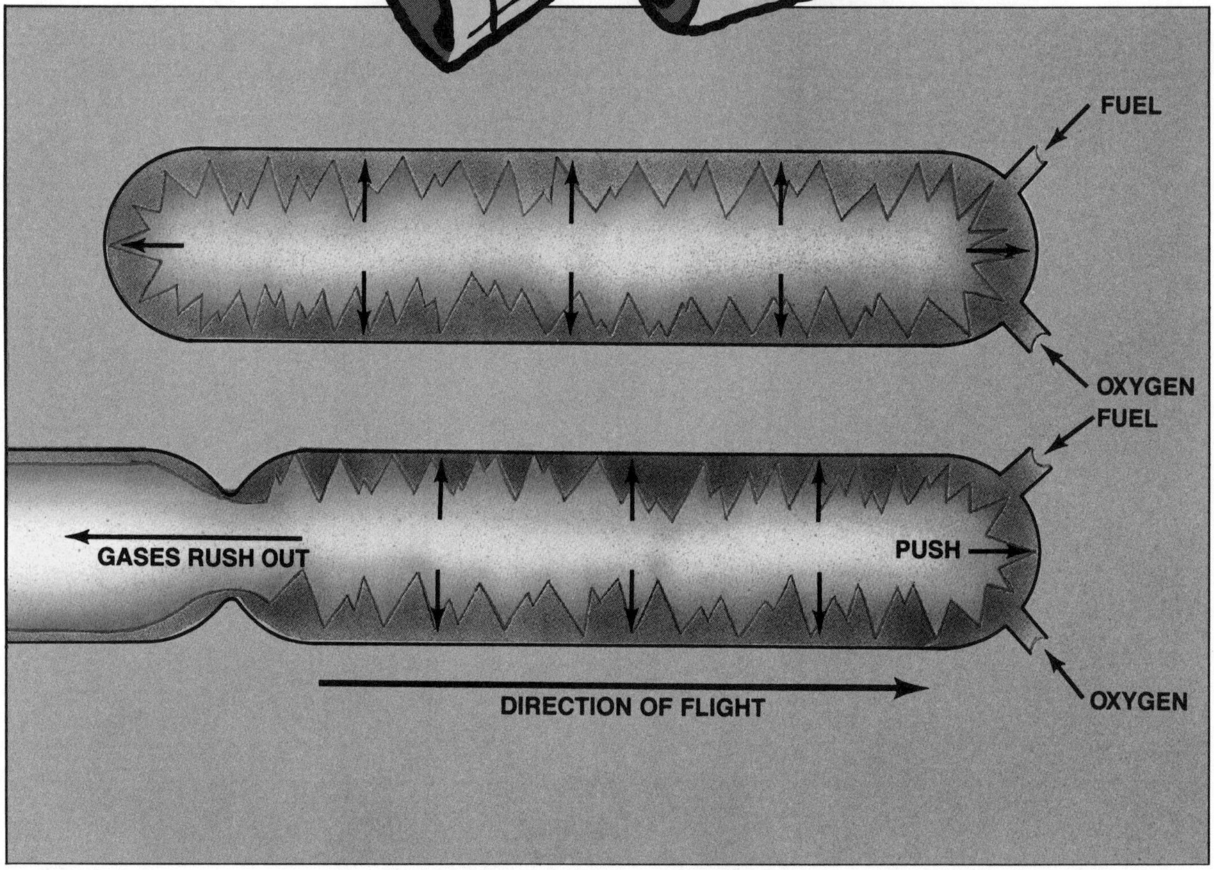

FUEL

OXYGEN

FUEL

GASES RUSH OUT

PUSH

DIRECTION OF FLIGHT

OXYGEN

ORBITS AND GRAVITY

What is an orbit?

The path of an object around another is called an orbit. The planets move in orbits around the Sun. The Moon orbits the Earth, and a spacecraft can orbit around and around the Earth. It's just like walking around a friend.

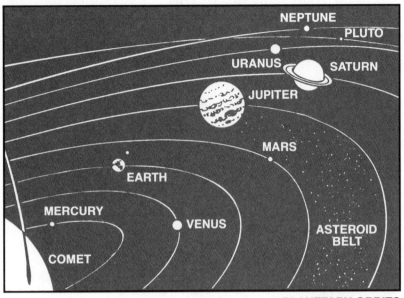

PLANETARY ORBITS

What is gravity?

Gravity is a force that every planet, star, and moon has. This force causes everything on or near the planet, star, or moon to be pulled toward its center.

The pull of the Earth's gravity holds the Moon in its orbit. The pull of the Sun's gravity keeps the planets in their orbits.

Stand on a bathroom scale. Suppose it shows you weigh 60 pounds. This means the downward pull of the Earth's gravity on your body measures 60 pounds.

How fast does a rocket need to travel to escape the Earth's gravity?

A rocket's escape speed must be 7 miles a second to get beyond the Earth's pull. That means the rocket is traveling 25,000 miles per hour!

How did rockets send early spacecraft into orbit?

This was done in two or three stages. Here's how a three-stage launch works.

First-stage rockets, sometimes called boosters, give the spacecraft a powerful push that lifts it from the ground. In two and a half minutes, the boosters have carried the spacecraft 40 miles. It is then going 6,000 miles an hour. At that time, the first-stage rockets stop firing and drop into the ocean.

Next, the second-stage rockets fire for six minutes. The spacecraft is now up about 100 miles, going more than 14,000 miles an hour. Then the second-stage rockets drop off.

The third-stage rockets are then fired for about two minutes. This gets the spacecraft to a height of 120 miles and a speed of about 17,500 miles an hour. The spacecraft has escaped the Earth's pull and gone into orbit around it. The third-stage rockets are left behind in outer space.

What happens to the parts of a spacecraft that are dropped off?

As a spacecraft goes up, objects such as rockets are sometimes left behind in space. The first rockets dropped are slowed down by the air. Some of these burn up as they fall. Others splash down into the ocean.

Once the spacecraft is outside the Earth's atmosphere, objects that are let loose go into orbit around the Earth. These objects are called space junk. They may orbit the Earth for a year or longer before they drop down and burn up. There are more than 3,000 pieces of space junk still in orbit.

HERE'S THE WORLD CLASS GOLF PRO SENDING A BALL INTO SPACE.

SPACECRAFT

What is the difference between a spacecraft and a spaceship?

The two words mean the same thing—any rocket-powered machine that can carry people or material into space. The word *spacecraft* is usually used in talking about a real rocket-powered craft. The word *spaceship* is used mainly in science-fiction.

How big is a spacecraft?

In the picture below you can see how large these different kinds of spacecraft are by comparing them with the size of the person. The Apollo spacecraft with its Saturn V rocket was 363 feet tall—as high as a 36-story building. It was built in 1968 and weighed more than 3,000 tons.

What kind of spacecraft did the first American astronauts use?

The first American, Alan Shepard, was sent into space in 1961 aboard a spacecraft in the Mercury program. The bell-shaped space capsule, which was less than seven feet wide, was big enough for only one person. It was pushed into space by a Redstone rocket.

What were Gemini spacecraft like?

Gemini spacecraft were used in the U.S. space program from 1964 to 1966. They were similar to those used in the Mercury program, but they could carry two people. Titan II rockets pushed these ten-foot-wide capsules into space.

APOLLO-SATURN V	APOLLO-SATURN 1B	SPACE SHUTTLE	GEMINI-TITAN II	MERCURY-ATLAS	MERCURY-REDSTONE	MAN
363 FEET	223 FEET	184 FEET	108 FEET	95 FEET	83 FEET	6 FEET

What were the next American spacecraft?

After the Gemini program, astronauts began using Apollo spacecraft. The Apollo program's first test flight was made in 1967. Although this was an unmanned flight, it cleared the way for a manned launch. The Apollo spacecraft differed from earlier spacecraft. They had three main parts—the command module, the service module, and the lunar module.

What is a command module?

A command module is the front end of an Apollo spacecraft, where the astronauts lived and did their work. This module is like the cockpit of an airplane. It is sometimes called a space capsule. You can see some of these command modules at the Smithsonian Institution in Washington, D.C.

What is a service module?

A service module is the part of an Apollo spacecraft that carried tanks of oxygen for the astronauts to breathe. It also held batteries for electric power needed to supply other important necessities, such as air-conditioning, heating, and lighting.

What is a spaceport?

A spaceport is a place on the Earth where spacecraft stay between trips. A spacecraft is loaded, repaired, and fueled at its spaceport.

The main American spaceport is located at the Kennedy Space Center in Florida.

Like an airport, a spaceport has hangars—huge buildings used to store the spacecraft. The spaceport also has large storage tanks for rocket fuel and lots of other equipment that astronauts need to travel in space.

How is a spacecraft steered?

This is usually done by firing the rocket motors that are at the bottom of the spacecraft. To turn the spacecraft just a little, special small rockets on the sides of the spacecraft are fired. These steering rockets can be worked by the astronauts or by radio signals from the ground.

APOLLO-SOYUZ DOCKING

APOLLO

SOYUZ

Astronaut Thomas Stafford meets Cosmonaut Aleksey Leonov.

What does the "docking" of two spacecraft mean?

Two spacecraft in orbit can meet and link together. They use their small rocket motors to line up. Then they slowly move toward each other until they can lock together, or dock.

In 1975, an American Apollo spacecraft and a Soviet Soyuz (SOY-ooz) spacecraft docked 138 miles above the Earth. There were cosmonauts—Soviet astronauts—aboard the Soyuz. The astronauts and the cosmonauts visited back and forth between the two spacecraft.

A space shuttle can open its doors to launch satellites.

THE SPACE SHUTTLE

What is a space shuttle?

Space shuttles are the more recent of the U.S. spacecraft. A shuttle is shaped like a huge airplane and is 185 feet long. It is able to orbit the Earth and then fly back through the atmosphere and land on a runway, just like an airplane. A space shuttle can be used many times—up to 100! Shuttles can't go into interplanetary space, but they bring us one step closer to building a spacecraft that could visit Mars or Venus.

Astronauts use space shuttles to perform experiments in space. The shuttles also carry things such as communication and television satellites.

When was the first space shuttle flight?

Columbia was the first manned shuttle to travel into space. It was launched on April 12, 1981. On that first flight, the shuttle orbited the Earth for two days and performed scientific experiments.

How are the shuttles moved from place to place on the Earth?

A craft the size of a space shuttle needs a special lift! When it has to be moved from one base to another, the spacecraft is attached to a large airplane. The plane gives the shuttle a piggyback ride to its new home.

NO, I WON'T GIVE YOU A PIGGYBACK RIDE TO SCHOOL TODAY.

Shuttle *Columbia* rides piggyback.

Does a shuttle have its own rockets?

Yes. A shuttle has two rocket boosters that help it break the Earth's gravity at lift-off. After that, the rockets fall off and drop into the ocean. Special ships pick up these rocket boosters and return them to the spaceport. They will be refueled and used on another mission.

A shuttle also has on-board rocket engines. These engines help it get into space, then they guide it. They also help the shuttle return to Earth by slowing it down. Once the shuttle has slowed, gravity pulls it into the atmosphere.

How many shuttle spacecraft are there?

Since 1981, four space shuttles have been built—*Columbia, Challenger, Discovery,* and *Atlantis.* Now that the *Challenger* is no longer flying, a new shuttle is being built. It will be called *Endeavour.*

Space shuttle *Discovery* counts down to lift-off.

Why is the *Challenger* shuttle no longer flying?

In 1986, the *Challenger* shuttle exploded just after it was launched. The seven people aboard the spacecraft were killed.

One member of the *Challenger* crew was a teacher named Christa McAuliffe. She was the first teacher selected to fly in space.

27

SATELLITES

A collection of images taken by the *Voyager 1* spacecraft, during its Saturn flyby in November, 1980.

What is a satellite?

Anything in space that moves in an orbit is called a satellite (SAT-uh-lite). The Earth is a satellite of the Sun. So are the other planets in our solar system because they orbit the Sun. The Moon is a satellite of the Earth because it orbits the Earth. Seven of the planets have satellites—or moons— moving around them. The Earth has only 1 moon, but Jupiter has 16. Saturn has 17! And more moons may be discovered orbiting the planets. These moons are called natural satellites.

There are also artificial (ahr-tuh-FISH-ull) satellites. The word *artificial* means "made by people." Artificial satellites are built on Earth and put into orbit. Since the beginning of the space age, hundreds of artificial satellites have been sent into space—weather satellites, TV satellites, communications satellites, and many other kinds.

What was the first satellite to orbit the Earth?

The Moon, of course! It is the Earth's natural satellite and has been orbiting the Earth for billions of years. The first artificial satellite to orbit the Earth, *Sputnik I*, was launched by the Soviet Union in 1957. *Sputnik I* gave us information about meteoroids and radiation. A few months later, the United States sent up its own satellite, *Explorer I*. It discovered one of the radiation belts around the Earth.

What do artificial satellites do?

There are different kinds of artificial satellites. Weather satellites orbit the Earth several hundred miles up. They measure the temperature and amount of moisture, or dampness, in the air. They send back TV pictures showing where there are clouds and storms on Earth.

Communications satellites pick up electrical waves from TV stations. The waves bounce back to distant places on the Earth. That is how you get live TV broadcasts from halfway around the world. Some communications satellites are used for sending long-distance telephone calls.

Other satellites help scientists gather information about outer space. These satellites measure radiation that does not get through the air to the ground. Some scientific satellites carry telescopes that send back pictures of planets and stars.

29

The word *astronaut* means "sailor among the stars." If you want to become an astronaut, you must be under 34 years old, intelligent, and in perfect health. You need to have a good education and go through a long testing and training period. Astronauts must study science and engineering and have at least 1,000 hours of experience flying jet airplanes. It takes a special person to make the grade in outer space!

THREE CHEERS FOR ASTRONAUTS

PREPARING ASTRONAUTS FOR SPACE TRAVEL

SPACE FLIGHT TRAINING

How are astronauts trained for space travel?

Scientists have set up labs on the Earth that copy the way astronauts will work, live, and feel when they are in space. For example, an astronaut is put inside a large metal ball. The ball is spun at high speed in order to put a great push on his or her body. This pressure is like the push the astronaut will feel when a spacecraft zooms upward.

Astronauts also train by moving around underwater in space suits. That helps them get used to the feeling of floating weightless—weighing in at zero pounds—in space. They also work in an exact copy of the spacecraft. In that way, they can practice using the buttons and switches that will control the spacecraft.

ASTRONAUTS IN OUTER SPACE

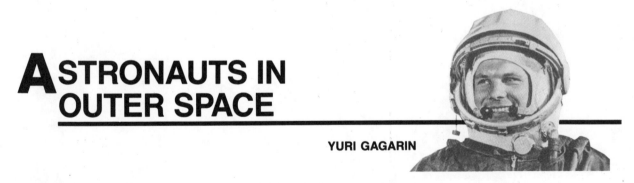

YURI GAGARIN

Who were the first astronauts?

The first person to fly around the Earth in outer space was a Soviet cosmonaut named Yury Gagarin (You-ree guh-GAH-rin). His flight, made in 1961, lasted a little less than two hours. Alan Shepard was the first American in space when he made a suborbital flight a few months later in his capsule, *Freedom 7*. John Glenn was the first American to orbit the Earth. His spacecraft, *Friendship 7*, circled the Earth three times during his five-hour flight, made in 1962.

Have women traveled in space?

Yes. The first woman in space was a Soviet cosmonaut named Valentina Tereshkova (val-en-TEEN-uh tay-resh-KOE-vah). She spent 71 hours in the Soviet spacecraft *Vostok 6*, which orbited the Earth in 1963.

VALENTINA TERESHKOVA

Who was the first American woman in space?

Dr. Sally Ride soared into space in a space shuttle in 1983. Americans were proud of their first woman in space. She is a top scientist and a fine athlete. Since then, other American women have traveled to outer space.

SALLY RIDE

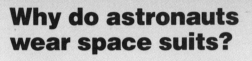

Why do astronauts wear space suits?

Space suits keep astronauts healthy and comfortable when they take a space walk or land on the Moon. Each suit is airtight. It keeps the air, the temperature, and the pressure inside the suit as normal as possible. The astronauts also wear helmets that have a gold coating on the front. This protects them from the ultraviolet rays of the Sun. Without the Earth's atmosphere to protect them, astronauts would get sunburned very fast.

Astronauts in the spacecraft wear everyday clothes.

Can astronauts take off their space suits during a trip?

Yes, if they stay inside the craft. They must suit up again before they take a space walk or land on the Moon. If they are going far from the spacecraft, they also hook up a jet pack, which holds life-support and communications equipment. When astronauts are inside the spacecraft, they wear everyday clothes.

33

Why do things float around in a spacecraft?

On the Earth, gravity holds everything down. While a spacecraft is orbiting, the Earth's gravity is still pulling on everything in the craft. But another force, which comes from orbiting, also pulls on everything. The two forces are equal and cause everything—and everyone—to float. This kind of floating is called weightlessness. Anything in the spacecraft that is not held down will float around.

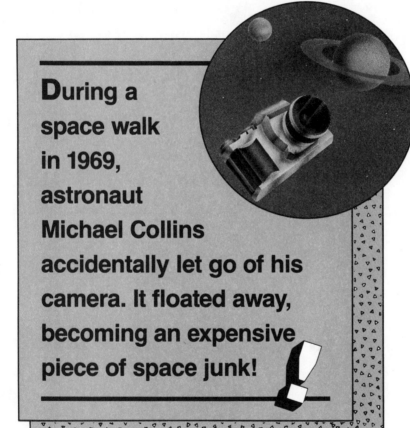

During a space walk in 1969, astronaut Michael Collins accidentally let go of his camera. It floated away, becoming an expensive piece of space junk!

What is a space walk?

When astronauts go outside their orbiting spacecraft, we say they are taking a space walk. Of course, they are not really walking. They are only drifting alongside the spacecraft. On early programs such as Mercury, a drifting astronaut was connected to the spacecraft by a long hose called a tether. The tether kept the astronaut from floating off into space. It had a tube that supplied the astronaut with oxygen so he could breathe, and it had electric lines for air-conditioning and radio. The space suit worn on shuttle missions today has all these things built right in!

What do astronauts eat?

Freeze-dried foods are used in flight to save space and to keep foods fresh. When food is freeze-dried, it is first frozen, then the ice that forms is taken out. The astronauts just add water to freeze-dried food, and it is ready to eat.

In an orbiting spacecraft, eating is tricky because of weightlessness. Astronauts cannot drink from an open cup because the liquid forms blobs that float around and wet anything they hit. So drinks must be kept in closed plastic bags. Astronauts must squeeze the liquid right into their mouths. Solid foods are in bite-sized pieces so that crumbs will not float around and pollute the air in the spacecraft.

On long trips in the future, astronauts may grow and harvest their own food plants in a special section of the spacecraft.

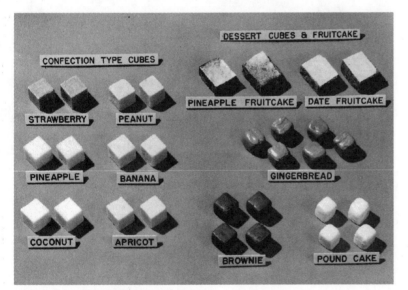

FREEZE-DRIED SPACE DESSERTS

How do astronauts get rid of body wastes?

Liquid waste is pumped into space, where it becomes a gas. Solid waste is put into plastic bags with chemicals that kill bacteria. The bags are thrown away upon return to Earth. On some space trips, all wastes are stored on board and then emptied upon return to Earth.

KEEPING ASTRONAUTS HEALTHY

What is space medicine?

It is the medical science that deals with the health of astronauts. Scientists want to know how space affects the health of space travelers. Doctors study the people being trained in labs on Earth. They also check the health of astronauts while they are in space and after they return to Earth.

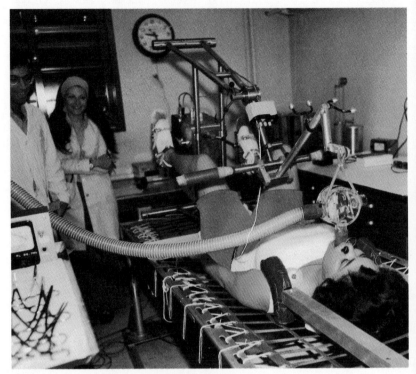
Doctors oversee the training of astronauts.

How do doctors check astronauts in space?

Electrical machines connected to the body of an astronaut check his or her breathing, heartbeat, and temperature. Readings are automatically sent back by radio to doctors on Earth.

What does space travel do to an astronaut's thoughts and feelings?

When an astronaut is alone in space for many, many days, the astronaut may become upset. He or she might even panic. Sometimes things look blurry. He or she may feel strange, and things around him or her may not seem real. However, there are always great things to keep an astronaut going. The astronaut is excited about the trip in space and knows how important the work is. Besides, the thrill of new discoveries makes space travel especially worthwhile!

CHAPTER 4

You've studied and trained. You've passed the tests. Now you're dressed in your space suit, and all systems are *go*. Where are you headed? You're about to take the trip of a lifetime. You're blasting off to outer space!

LIFT-OFF AND LANDING

NASA'S MISSION CONTROL NASA

What is NASA?

NASA, the National Aeronautics and Space Administration, is the part of the United States Government that is in charge of exploring space. Thousands of space experts, scientists, and engineers work for NASA.

MISSION CONTROL IN HOUSTON, TEXAS

How does NASA keep track of a traveling spacecraft?

In the past, radio signals from the spacecraft were picked up by tracking stations on the Earth. These stations were located in several places around the world.

NASA is now replacing most tracking stations with satellites that are in orbit more than 22,000 miles up. They can do the same work the ground stations did, but in addition, a space shuttle is almost always in sight of these tracking satellites. The signals from the satellites are sent into a computer at mission control, which uses the information to tell scientists where the spacecraft is.

What is mission control?

All space flights are run from a center called mission control, which is located in Houston, Texas. The people in charge of the flight work at this center.

The people at mission control talk with the astronauts by radio, and they watch signal lights and special TV screens and computers to keep track of the flight.

3–2–1 BLAST OFF!

What is a countdown?

A countdown is a check-up time before a space-craft is launched from the Earth. During this time, every inch of the rocket and spacecraft is tested to see that it works. All the machinery that sets off and guides the craft is tested, too. A green light is switched on for each part that is in good working order. If something is not working, the countdown stops until that part is fixed. A person speaking over a loudspeaker at the spaceport announces how many hours and minutes of countdown are left before lift-off.

A countdown may take hours—or even days. It will continue until all the controls flash a green light. Finally, the loudspeaker booms, "10–9–8–7–6–5–4–3–2–1—ignition! We have lift-off." With a loud roar, the rockets blast off and the spacecraft begins to rise.

Why is an astronaut sometimes strapped to a seat in the spacecraft?

An astronaut is strapped to his or her seat only during lift-off and return to Earth. At those times, the astronaut's body feels a great push. It is the same kind of push that you feel when you ride in a car that makes a sudden, fast start. It seems that you are being shoved back into your seat.

The pushing forces are much, much stronger in a spacecraft that is leaving or coming back to Earth. The astronaut in a space shuttle feels a force of nearly three times his own body weight! That is why he must be supported by a seat during take-off and landing.

3 - 2 - 1 Lift off!
A space shuttle
blasts off.

COMING BACK TO EARTH

What is re-entry?

As a spacecraft returns from outer space, it must plunge into the air before it can land. Coming back into the Earth's atmosphere is called re-entry.

What is the heat shield on a spacecraft?

When returning spacecraft plunge back into the Earth's air, they get extremely hot from friction, a kind of rubbing and scraping of the spacecraft against the air. To protect the astronauts, the spacecraft is covered with a heat shield. Temperatures on the heat shield reach about 5,000 degrees Fahrenheit. Some of the plastic melts and burns off, taking away the dangerous heat. Inside the craft, the temperature stays at 80 degrees Fahrenheit.

A spacecraft encounters the heat of friction.

Can the astronauts talk with mission control during landing?

Astronauts and mission control talk back and forth by radio right up to the time the spacecraft comes back into the atmosphere. Then, as the heat shield begins to get hot, a strange thing happens. The air around the spacecraft becomes superheated. This is caused by friction of the spacecraft against the air. Radio waves cannot get through this superheated air. So, for several minutes, there is only silence between the astronauts and the ground.

How did manned spacecraft before space shuttles make a safe landing?

The Mercury, Gemini, and Apollo spacecraft all re-entered in much the same way. The Mercury and Gemini and the command module of the Apollo spacecraft all had thick, heavy heat shields on the rear of the spacecraft.

Before re-entry, the capsule was turned around so that the end with the heat shield faced forward. This was done by firing small steering rockets. The capsule had to enter the atmosphere tilted in a slanting path.

At the time of re-entry, the Apollo capsule could move at 25,000 miles per hour. For a safe landing, this speed had to be cut down to only a few miles an hour. About four miles above the Earth, two small parachutes were opened to slow the falling capsule. About two miles up, three big parachutes were opened. The capsule then floated to Earth at a safe speed.

APOLLO 16 SPLASHDOWN

What was a splashdown?

A splashdown was the moment a space capsule landed in the Earth's water. Astronauts used to land this way. After splashdown, ships and helicopters rushed to the floating capsule. Divers jumped into the water and placed a doughnut-shaped balloon around the capsule to make sure it did not sink. The astronauts opened a door and were lifted into a helicopter. They were then taken to a nearby ship.

Scuba divers who assisted astronauts after splashdown were called para-rescuemen.

Some Soviet cosmonauts were ejected from their spacecraft—and floated to Earth in their own parachutes! After they were ejected, retro-rockets were used to slow down the landing craft!

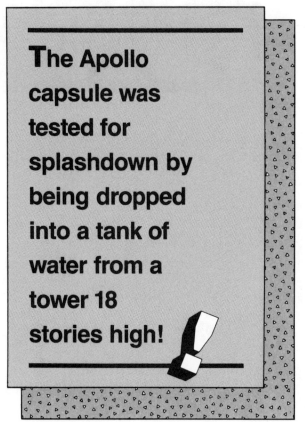

The Apollo capsule was tested for splashdown by being dropped into a tank of water from a tower 18 stories high!

How do the space shuttles land?

Space shuttles do not splash down in the ocean. A shuttle lands like an airplane, gliding down a runway. However, as it enters the Earth's atmosphere, it must be protected from the heat of re-entry. The outside of the craft is covered with special silicone tiles that keep it from burning up.

CHAPTER 5

After thousands of years of gazing at the Moon from the Earth, it finally happened. On July 20, 1969, an American spacecraft called *Apollo* landed there. For the first time in history, a person walked on the Moon! That person was Neil Armstrong.

TAKE A WALK ON THE MOON

THE FIRST MOON EXPLORERS

What did Neil Armstrong say when he first landed on the Moon?

"Houston, Tranquility Base here. The Eagle has landed," were the first words spoken by astronaut Neil Armstrong. We usually remember the words he said when he took the first step on the Moon: "That's one small step for a man, one giant leap for mankind."

APOLLO 11 CREW

Who were the other astronauts on the first Moon voyage?

Another Apollo astronaut, Edwin "Buzz" Aldrin, also walked on the Moon. There was a third astronaut on that flight. His name was Michael Collins. He stayed aboard the Apollo command module as it orbited the Moon.

A human footprint on the Moon.

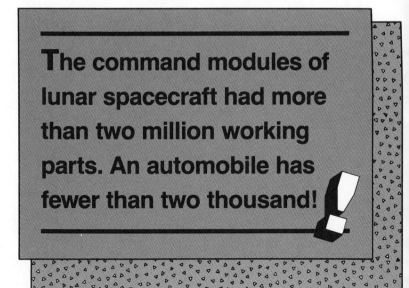

The command modules of lunar spacecraft had more than two million working parts. An automobile has fewer than two thousand!

44

© 1988 United Feature Syndicate, Inc.

How long does a spacecraft take to go to the Moon and back?

The first manned flight to the Moon took about four days from the time the spacecraft left the Earth until it went into orbit around the Moon. The return trip took a little less than three days.

Have there been other manned landings on the Moon?

Yes. There have been five more landings since the first one in 1969. In all, a dozen people, all Americans, have walked on the Moon.

Astronaut David Scott salutes from the Moon.

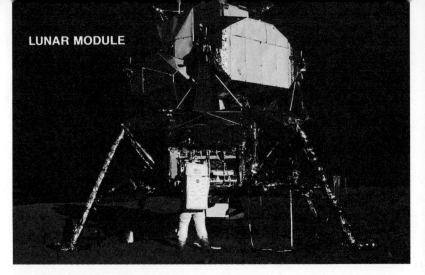

LUNAR MODULE

How did the astronauts get down to the Moon's surface from their spacecraft?

Two astronauts boarded a special separate spacecraft called a lunar module, which they had brought with them from Earth. Usually called the LM (pronounced LEM), the lunar module was carried into Earth's orbit attached to the third stage of the Saturn V rocket. Then it was attached to the nose of the command module for the trip to the Moon. After the spacecraft went into orbit around the Moon, the LM separated from it and was lowered to the Moon's surface. One astronaut stayed behind to operate the command module.

When the LM approached the Moon, rockets were fired to control its descent. These rockets helped the craft make a soft landing.

How did the astronauts get back to their spacecraft when they were ready to leave the Moon?

When the astronauts finished their Moon work, they climbed back into the LM and fired up its rockets. The LM flew up and met the command module that was orbiting the Moon. The two craft docked and the astronauts boarded the command module. The LM was then released. Rather than carry the heavy LM back to Earth, the astronauts left it behind. Then the rockets on the spacecraft were fired, and it headed back toward Earth.

How did the astronauts talk to each other on the Moon?

Outer space has no air to carry sound waves. Because there is no air on the Moon, there is no sound. Astronauts had to use a small radio that was built into each space suit to talk to each other. Radios can work on the Moon because radio waves can travel even where there is no air.

THERE'S A FULL EARTH TONIGHT!

GETTING AROUND ON THE MOON

Is there gravity on the Moon?

Yes. But the Moon is much smaller than the Earth, so its gravity is much weaker. The pull of gravity on the Moon is about one-sixth that of the gravity here on Earth.

If you weigh 60 pounds on Earth, you would weigh only 10 pounds on the Moon!

Apollo astronaut Edwin "Buzz" Aldrin, Jr., walks on the surface of the Moon.

Why did astronauts shuffle along instead of walk on the Moon?

The Moon's gravity does not pull as strongly as the Earth's gravity. If the astronauts had tried to walk the way they do on Earth, they would have risen a few feet off the ground with every step. They were able to keep better control and stay on the ground by just shuffling along. If astronauts on the Moon did not have to wear their heavy space suits and jet packs, they would be able to jump 35 feet high!

What did the astronauts leave on the Moon the first time they traveled there?

Neil Armstrong and Buzz Aldrin of the *Apollo 11* mission left human footprints, a U.S. flag, and a sign that read: "They came in peace for all mankind." They also left a package of scientific instruments, including a laser reflector, a solar wind experiment, and an instrument to record lunar quakes.

Athletes on the Moon would be able to leap over a two-story house. They would come down no harder than they do after a six-foot jump on Earth!

What did the astronauts bring back home?

They brought back rock samples for scientists to study. Astronauts have collected 55 pounds of Moon rocks!

LUNAR ROVER

How did astronauts get around on the Moon?

Some astronauts were able to ride on the Moon in style in a moon rover. The rover looks like a jeep or a dune buggy. It was specially built because the surface of the Moon is very rough and rocky. The moon rover gets its power from batteries. On one Moon expedition in 1971, astronauts David Scott and James Irwin traveled more than 17 miles in their moon rover. They explored new parts of the Moon and collected more rocks. A moon rover was used again in April 1972 by the *Apollo 16* crew. A rover was also used by the *Apollo 17* crew in December 1972.

CHAPTER 6

The next time you're outside on a clear night, take a look at the sky. How far away the Moon looks! It's hard to believe that astronauts have traveled there. Will men ever visit faraway planets? Scientists say yes!

GET SET FOR THE FUTURE

SPACE PROBES

What is a space probe?

A space probe is an un-manned vehicle launched to explore the solar system. A space probe can either fly past a moon or a planet or land on it. Probes help scientists find out about the climates and surfaces of those faraway places. Before astronauts blasted off to the Moon, scientists used space probes to discover whether the Moon's surface was hard enough to support a space-craft with people in it. And probes have told scientists that Neptune's surface swirls with stormy gases.

This space shuttle sent the *Magellan* probe (shown at top) to study Venus.

Where have space probes traveled?

Space probes have traveled millions, even billions, of miles into space. The *Pioneer 10* space probe and its twin, *Pioneer 11*, launched in 1972, were the first objects made by people to leave our solar system. During their voyages, they passed Jupiter and Saturn. *Voyager 1* and *Voyager 2* were launched in 1977. Both also flew by Jupiter and Saturn, but *Voyager 2* then went on to Uranus and Neptune before it, too, headed out of the solar system. After 12 years in space, *Voyager 2* was still sending information back to Earth!

Other probes, *Viking 1* and *Viking 2*, landed on Mars in 1976. They sent back the first photos taken from the surface of Mars.

Two space probes, called *Magellan* and *Galileo*, were launched in 1989. *Magellan* will orbit Venus. It will measure the atmosphere on Venus and tell us what its surface is like. *Galileo* is scheduled to reach Jupiter in 1995.

VISITING OTHER PLANETS

Will people ever be able to land on other planets?

Many scientists think that someday we'll be able to send astronauts to another planet. The exciting information we receive from space probes makes many people eager to visit other planets.

Which planet would astronauts visit?

Probably Mars. It's the second closest planet to Earth, and it's farther away from the Sun. It's very cold, so astronauts would have to wear special space suits to keep them warm.

Venus is the closest planet to Earth, but it's very hot there. Temperatures on the surface are higher than 800 degrees Fahrenheit. It would be hard for astronauts to live in that kind of heat.

SPACE STATIONS AND COLONIES

What is a space station?

A space station is a special kind of satellite that orbits the Earth a few hundred miles up. Astronauts live and work in it. The first American space station was *Skylab*, launched in 1973. Three different crews spent time in *Skylab*. The last crew stayed in space for almost three months and returned to Earth in 1974. While they were there, the astronauts performed many experiments. One was to take measurements of the Earth and the Sun with a giant telescope.

Skylab orbited the Earth until 1979. Its orbit weakened, and it dropped low enough into the Earth's atmosphere to burn up.

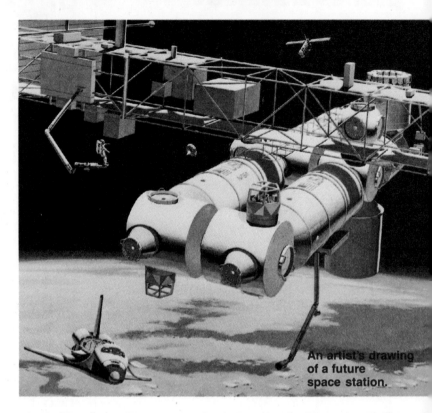
An artist's drawing of a future space station.

Will there be other space stations?

Yes. One is now being designed, and the first parts are scheduled to go into space in 1995 or 1996. It will be very large. Astronauts will have to build it in space with parts sent up from the Earth—with the help of space shuttles.

The station will spin, or rotate, as it orbits the Earth. This motion will create a pull similar to that of Earth's gravity. With this gravity, people will be able to walk around the space station, instead of being weightless and floating.

What will new space stations be used for?

Scientists will use new space stations to conduct more experiments in space. American astronauts have already discovered the incredible possibilities of working in space. With zero gravity and no air in space labs, nearly perfect scientific experiments can be performed. Such experiments might help us create new drugs to cure many diseases.

A space station can also be a rest stop for astronauts before they head farther out into space. With science labs, dormitories, kitchens, and even a gym inside the space station, astronauts and scientists will be able to perform many activities.

A company that makes soft drinks has already designed a machine to sell soda in a space station!

GYM

How long can people live in space?

So far, the longest space mission took place on the Soviet space station *Mir* in 1987. Two cosmonauts spent 366 days—one day more than a year!—in space. They traveled more than a million miles during that time.

Astronauts aboard a space station perform many scientific experiments.

Will there ever be factories in space?

Yes! In space factories, we could make some things that are hard to make on Earth. For example, metals can be joined together by heating them. This is called welding. A weld is stronger if it's not touched by air while the welder is working. Welding would be easier in a factory where there is no air—on a space station orbiting the Earth.

What is a space colony?

There are no space colonies yet. But when they're built, they will be like islands in space where thousands of people can live and work. Each space colony will be different. One, designed like a huge tube about half a mile long, will orbit the Earth. Like space stations, the tube will rotate slowly to give the feeling of gravity. Large mirrors will focus the Sun's rays and provide power for electricity in the colony. Once the colony is set up, people could raise their own food in space.

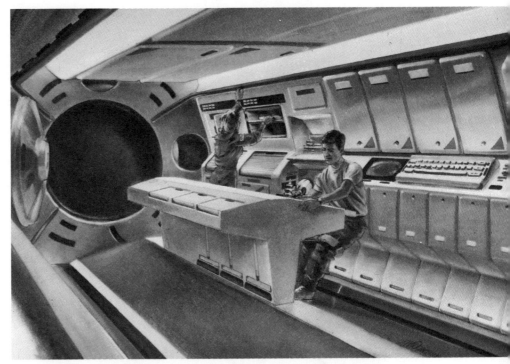

This might be a typical kitchen in the space station of the future.

Will people ever live on the Moon?

Scientists are talking about building a space station on the Moon. A lunar settlement would give astronauts a place to explore and experiment. It would also be a resting place for astronauts before they go on to visit faraway planets.

"Eyes on the Stars"

Laika the wonder dog

A dog named Laika was the first space traveler. Laika was sent up in a Soviet spacecraft in 1957, before the first humans explored space. Laika proved that living animals could survive in space.

Feeling taller?

An astronaut can grow an inch or two taller on a long space mission. Because there is no gravity in space, the bones in an astronaut's spine can move apart slightly. But when the astronaut returns to Earth, gravity will soon shrink the astronaut back to his or her normal size.

The Snoopy Space Award

NASA astronauts give out a very special prize, the Silver Snoopy medal. This award is given to people who work hard in the space program. Snoopy has been a friend to astronauts since 1969 when *Apollo 10*'s lunar module was named after him. What was the command module code-named? Charlie Brown, of course!

MANNED MISSIONS TO REMEMBER

May 5, 1961.
Alan B. Shepard becomes the first American in space when he makes a suborbital flight for the Mercury program in his capsule, *Freedom 7*.

Astronaut Ed White takes a space walk.

John Glenn, Jr., entering the *Friendship 7*.

June 3, 1965.
Astronaut Edward H. White II takes the first American space walk. Astronaut James A. McDivitt stays in the two-man Gemini spacecraft with the hatch open while White floats a short distance away. He is connected to Gemini by a tether.

February 20, 1962.
John H. Glenn, Jr., makes three full orbits of the Earth in his Mercury program capsule, *Friendship 7*.

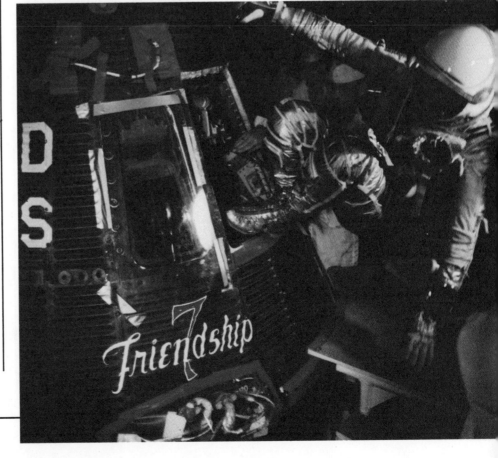

December 21, 1968.
Apollo 8's three-man crew (Frank Borman, James A. Lovell, Jr., William A. Anders) becomes the first to orbit the Moon.

December 15, 1965.
Astronauts Walter M. Schirra, Jr., and Thomas P. Stafford, in the *Gemini 6-A* capsule, hold the first meeting in space! Their craft docks with another spacecraft, *Gemini 7*, piloted by Frank Borman and James A. Lovell, Jr.

July 16, 1969.
At last, men reach the Moon! *Apollo 11* lifts off on July 16, 1969, and astronauts Neil A. Armstrong and Edwin E. "Buzz" Aldrin pilot a lunar module to the surface of the Moon on July 20. They go outside in their space suits and walk on the Moon for five hours.

GEMINI 7
APOLLO 11 LIFT-OFF

July 26, 1971.
Crew members David R. Scott; Alfred M. Worden, Jr.; and James B. Irwin ride in style! *Apollo 15* is the first space mission to use the moon rover to travel on the Moon.

May 14, 1973.
Skylab is launched into orbit. It is America's first manned space station.

July 15, 1975.
American astronauts Thomas P. Stafford, Donald K. Slayton, and Vance D. Brand use their Apollo spacecraft to dock with a Soviet Soyuz craft in space.

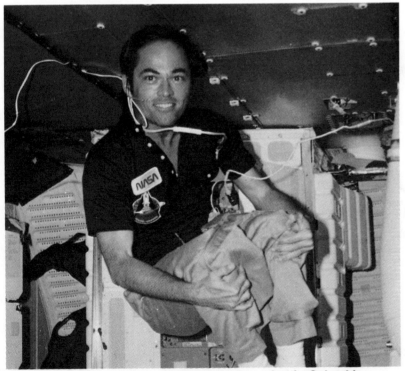

Astronaut Robert Crippen aboard the space shuttle *Columbia.*

April 1981–present.
The world's first reusable spacecraft, NASA's fleet of space shuttles, make numerous trips into space.

◆ IN THE ◆
NEXT VOLUME

Have you ever wondered what an octopus does with all those arms, or how fireflies light up, or whether electric eels really make electricity? You can find the answers to these questions and lots more in volume 4, *Creatures of Land and Sea—Wild, Weird, and Wonderful.*